The Team

Mick Dennis is a freelance journalist and media consultant who is the *Daily Express*'s football correspondent. He has worked as sports editor of the *Evening Standard* and for five national newspapers. In his spare time, he is a football referee, vice chair of a charitable trust which manages local sports facilities and a magistrate. He lives in Hemel Hempstead.

The Team

Mick Dennis

CORGI BOOKS

THE TEAM
A CORGI BOOK: 0 552 15372 9
9780552153720

First publication in Great Britain

PRINTING HISTORY
Corgi edition published 2006

1 3 5 7 9 10 8 6 4 2

Set in Stone Serif by SX Composing DTP, Rayleigh, Essex

Corgi Books are published by Transworld Publishers,
61–63 Uxbridge Road, London W5 5SA,
a division of The Random House Group Ltd,
in Australia by Random House Australia (Pty) Ltd,
20 Alfred Street, Milsons Point, Sydney, NSW 2061, Australia,
in New Zealand by Random House New Zealand Ltd,
18 Poland Road, Glenfield, Auckland 10, New Zealand
and in South Africa by Random House (Pty) Ltd,
Isle of Houghton, Corner of Boundary Road & Carse
O'Gowrie, Houghton 2198, South Africa.

Printed and bound in Great Britain by
Bookmarque Ltd, Croydon, Surrey

Papers used by Transworld Publishers are natural, recyclable products made from wood grown in sustainable forests. The manufacturing processes conform to the environmental regulations of the country of origin.

Foreword

I know extremely intelligent people who read little, or not at all. I know much less intelligent people who read, perhaps not too much, but a great deal. And then there are intelligent people who read a lot, and less intelligent people who read little or not at all.

There are those who claim to know the truth, as if there were such a thing as absolute truth. I believe everyone has their own truth, and that there are no absolutes. Should one be happy with one's own truth, or exchange ideas with others, even at the risk of losing one's own truth or being enriched (not in the material sense) by the other's truth? No one possesses the absolute truth, not even me. I'm just trying to write down what I think about the importance of reading.

The act of reading should enrich us. It should not make us think we are clever, or make us look down on anyone.

If it is necessary to read, then, it is also important to know why we are reading, who we are, and what the meaning of our existence is.

Reading in order to quote extracts from what one has read is not, it seems to me, a good reason for reading. Reading for inspiration without losing oneself in the process is a good reason for reading. Reading to learn and in order to enrich one's life without losing oneself in the process is another. Reading to stay informed. Reading to escape reality by entering into a world created by the author. Reading for the love of suspense. Reading to discover. To laugh. To cry. To relax. To give birth, because passion can be born from reading. Reading to admire or to be influenced. I could list hundreds of reasons for reading.

Need I list each and every one? Perhaps one day someone will do it, and maybe some of those who today read little or not at all will read that list. Because just as a passion can be born from reading, the passion for reading itself can be born too. At any age. But there has to be a beginning, one day or another.

Some people don't read – or not very much. But they know how to listen to what others have said. And reading is just another way of knowing what others have said.

Of course it is possible to exist without reading. Just as one can exist without being able to read. But even without considering essays, novels, short stories, poetry, biographies, magazines, broadsheet or tabloid newspapers, is it not necessary, for the sake of one's own independence, to be able to read in order to understand official letters and fill in forms correctly?

Well, maybe if it is an official letter or form one would happily not read. But one does have to deal with an official letter or form. And to do so one has to read. In order to deal with them – to write – reading is necessary. Even if just a little.

But there are exceptions to everything.

If someone wanted to read in a different way, whether out of curiosity or because of being blind, they could also read braille. Whatever the method of reading, it promotes intellectual and emotional independence, which one does not have without reading. And if one is independent, one is better placed to help others to develop their intellectual and emotional or other potential.

Or perhaps I should have written something about reading palms.

Eric Cantona

Introduction

MY CAREER AS A Sunday footballer was summed up by a friend in four words: 'Could have been quicker.'

I was always very keen though. I spent hours learning to kick with both feet. I should have tried doing it one foot at a time, I suppose. OK, I lacked skill as well as pace, but I loved the game, and still do. I watch football every chance I get. I've coached teams, and for more than a decade I have refereed. Well, somebody has to.

I have also been lucky enough to make my living by writing about football. I've done so for five national newspapers. So when the idea of this book was put to me I jumped at it – which was a bit like how I used to tackle. It gave me the chance to talk to eleven football folk, all very different people doing different jobs.

They range from the bloke who knocked down the Liverpool Kop stand to a girl who dresses up as a big, blue lion. There's one current footballer, a lad who hopes to be a top player, and a man coming to terms with the end of his career. There's also a manager, a referee, a famous fan, a man who has been in your living room (via TV), and a chief exec who seldom goes to his own home. By talking to them all, and glimpsing their lives, I was able to look at football from eleven different and revealing angles. I had a ball.

So I must thank Phil French who, before he left the Premier League, helped set up the project, and Chris Hurst, who drove the whole book along for the Premier League. Doug Young at Transworld was a huge help as well. But most of all I thank the people in this book for letting me, and you, peer into their lives. They were very patient. Not one of them looked at his or her watch after our meeting and said, 'Could have been quicker.'

CHAPTER ONE

Adrian Chiles, Supporter

ONE DAY IN LONDON, a tramp walked up to Adrian Chiles. 'He was in a terrible state,' Adrian said. 'Very dirty and very rough. He looked as if he was going to talk to me. So I got ready to give him some money, but he put his arm around me and said, "I'm sorry, but the Albion have had it this season." Even down-and-outs feel sorry for me because I support West Brom.'

Everyone knows that Adrian is a West Bromwich Albion fan. It is such a big part of his life that he cannot hide it when he is fronting shows on BBC TV and radio. Not that he wants to hide it. 'I look at other sports, other people, and probably all of life in terms of my support for the Albion,' he said. 'I have this passion for the Albion, and if other people have a passion –

for another club, another sport, or almost anything – then they are all right by me. I don't care what it is they have a passion for, I just want them to have a passion.'

The BBC website lists his interests as child-care, his wife, West Bromwich Albion, golf and cooking, in that order. But his wife, BBC radio's Jane Garvey, is not sure she really comes before the football. Then again, not much does with Adrian. That is why he and I get on.

We first met through our jobs and soon realized we were both mad football fans. I can't explain why Adrian is such a devoted fan, because I can't explain why I am. When my team, Norwich City, lost in the play-off final against Birmingham in Cardiff in 2002, I went through every possible emotion. At the end I was so drained I could not think. I certainly could not talk. All for a football match – a game. No wonder the word 'fan' comes from 'fanatic'.

But enough about me. Back to Adrian – an utter fanatic. For this book, we met at his home, which is near BBC Television Centre in west London. Above the front door of the Chiles house is a stained-glass picture of a bird. It's a throstle – the West Brom bird.

Adrian's first job for the BBC was as a business reporter, and when Radio Five Live started in 1994 he had an early-morning spot called *Wake Up to Money*. But instead, listeners found themselves waking up to the Albion. 'Because I love the Albion, somehow I would end up talking about them all the time instead of business stuff,' Adrian said. 'In the end Five Live asked me to do a couple of football phone-ins when someone was on holiday. So I stopped doing the early-morning business stuff. Then the BBC gave me a Saturday morning show which was called *Weekend Breakfast* at first. It was not meant to be a football show at all. It was meant to be about life and cooking. But we did more and more sport and more and more football. In the end, without us really saying anything, it became a sports show.'

Because he was (and is) a mad fan, Adrian wanted to know everything about football. The show talked to people like the kit woman at Leeds. How did she keep the shirts and shorts white? And when football clubs first started buying so many players from abroad, Adrian's show had a chat with the man Coventry hired to translate things into different languages. He said the hardest bit was working out what was said by the manager, Gordon Strachan. Years later, Adrian worked with Strachan on *Match of the Day 2* on Sunday nights. Then the whole country had trouble working out what Strachan was saying.

It was Adrian's Saturday morning radio show which led to him getting that *Match of the Day 2* job, and a phone-in on Radio Five Live on Wednesday evenings. But the work has never stopped him going to the Albion. 'With the phone-in, I said to them, "Look, the reason you want to do this is because I am the sort of bloke who goes to matches, so it would be daft to stop me going to matches." So if the Albion are playing midweek, we do the phone-in from the ground after the game.

'On Saturdays, before we had kids, Jane came with me to games. So when I was doing the Saturday radio show, I'd leave the house at seven in the morning and Jane would be waiting outside with the car after the show. We went to games together. When we had kids she stopped coming, but I still go to games and don't get back until seven at night. It has caused a few rows.'

Adrian still makes non-sport programmes for TV, including BBC2's business programme *Working Lunch*, but West Brom are never far from his mind. 'On Saturdays, if I can't get to an away game for any reason, I go into the *Working Lunch* office and watch the BBC's pictures of the match on a TV on my desk. I go with a mate. This big, open-plan office is empty except for us two idiots staring at this screen and cheering the Albion.

'Most TV, radio and newspaper reporters are not fans with a passion for one club. To get to the top they have to stop going to see their team at quite an early age. That didn't happen with me, and I think other fans sort of understand that I am one of them. I wear my heart on my sleeve, but they sort of respect that. They understand my passion. And they know that I understand their passion. I care so much about the Albion that it is hard doing the job sometimes. If the Albion have lost – and it does happen – I can't bring myself to watch football on Saturday night at all. I should do. I'm not really doing my job by missing it, but I can't watch.

'One time, when I was doing the phone-in on

a Sunday, I was in the studio getting ready for the show and the Albion were playing at Fulham. I was watching Sky TV pictures and listening to Five Live's coverage. The radio was a few seconds ahead of the pictures. Right at the end, Fulham got a corner, and as they lined up to take it on the TV, the radio told me that they had scored. I still watched the TV hoping that the ball wouldn't go in the net. But it did, of course, and we lost. When I started the phone-in show that night I said, "Phone in quick because I might do something daft." I got in trouble about that when I got home because my wife was bathing the kids with the radio on and the girls wanted to know what Daddy was going to do which was daft.'

Adrian's job has taken him closer to his club than most fans get to theirs. 'The job has given me a glimpse behind the scenes,' he said. 'I know the chairman now, and I knew Gary Megson when he was manager. When the chairman and Gary fell out it was difficult. I had to write a piece for a newspaper and found it hard.'

Because Adrian has a well-known face, I wondered if it was also hard for him to be just one of the crowd at Albion.

'No,' he replied. 'I have a very small, nice type of fame which I don't mind at all. At the Albion everyone knows me, but I embrace that. I am just part of one big family. It is just bliss. Absolute bliss. I am not a bawler or a shouter. I just go very quiet and try to get through it. But when Albion stayed up [in the Premier League] on the very last day of the 2004/05 season so many people wanted to hug me. It was great to share the bliss I felt with all of them.'

Perhaps that is part of what being a fan is about. Belonging. Perhaps it is about sharing good times as well as bad times with other people. But perhaps we should not try too hard to understand what it's all about. You either know, from your own experiences, or you don't. Lots of people do seem to understand, though, and that is why they like Adrian. 'People come up to me all the time – and not just tramps. Strangers seem to be happy when I am really happy and seem to want to say something when they know I am hurting because the Albion have lost.'

But there was one time when he wanted to be less famous. 'Frank Skinner is really well-known and another Albion fan,' Adrian explained. 'He has to be so careful how he behaves because cameras are on him all the time at matches. When he was a guest on *Match of the Day 2*, the plan was for me to go to the game with him – Villa against the Albion – and then do the show. But I have WBA on my numberplate and I thought it would be a bit much, me and him driving up to the big car park at Villa with WBA on the car. So the BBC hired another car for me. When it turned up, it was a Skoda. Typical BBC.

Then, when we got to the game, I had to meet the bloke who is the West Brom mascot, Baggie Bird. I was going to run the London Marathon in the bird costume for charity and needed to try it on. I met the mascot outside the ground. At that point Frank said, "You know you were trying to protect us? Well, we're outside Villa, and now you are dressing up as Baggie Bird. Not really a low profile, is it?" He had a point.'

CHAPTER TWO

Craig Gardner, Academy Player

LET'S START WITH SOME numbers. In England, about five million children play football at school. But there are only twenty Premier League clubs. So, for most of the kids who kick a ball about at school and dream of playing in the Premier League, that is all it will ever be – a dream.

It is tougher to get to the top of the game in this country than it is in any other sport because so many people play it.

If you are pretty good at rowing, for instance, you will go far. Well, if you're rowing in the right direction, anyway. But in football, you have to be really special to have any chance at all of getting anywhere near the top of the game.

Here are some more numbers. In the season in which I visited the Aston Villa training ground to talk to Craig Gardner, Villa used twenty-two players in Premier League matches. Of those twenty-two, only seven had 'come through the ranks' at Villa, scrapping their way up from youth teams to the senior side. Villa had men from all over the world – from Europe, South America and Africa – but only seven from their own training scheme. And Villa are much better than most at giving local lads a chance. They scour the schools and Sunday League teams. They watch every match between district teams. Anyone with promise is invited for a trial. But they are also scouring the rest of the world to find players.

Here is one final gloomy set of numbers: three out of every four sixteen-year-olds on the books of pro clubs will be out of the game by the time they are twenty. No wonder, then, that if I had to pick one word to describe Craig, it would be 'anxious'. He was anxious about talking to me, anxious to please, anxious about saying the right things – and, above all else, anxious about his career.

Craig was eighteen when we talked, a clean-cut young man with an athlete's toned frame. He had played several games in midfield for the reserves but was still an 'academy boy' – a lad at the Aston Villa academy, which is a sort of football finishing school. 'I know it could all end tomorrow,' he said. 'And of course I don't want that to happen. That feeling is there all the time. When I first came to Villa for a trial, and trained and played with other lads, I knew that if I didn't do very, very well, it would all be over before it had started. Now, when I play a game, I know I have to do well because the coaches and everyone are looking at me, making decisions about me.'

The twin threats, the ever-present fears, are loss of form and injury. Craig dreads the first and has suffered the second. 'If I have a bad game, it's, it's . . .' His voice trailed off and he screwed his eyes shut, as if in terrible pain. 'I just go home and don't talk. It's terrible, really terrible. You know when you've had a bad game. Well, I do, and you just feel terrible. You think you have messed up everything. Terrible.'

And the injury? 'I was playing against MK Dons and just did an ordinary block tackle. I just felt my knee go. I tried to carry on with it, but I couldn't. I honestly didn't think it would be too bad, you know, but when I had all the tests and stuff they told me what I'd done.' He had torn his medial ligaments. They are on the side of the knee, and they hold the joint together. 'Even then, I didn't really think it would keep me out for long, but I was in plaster for twelve days and then I had a brace on for a week after that. For nine weeks I couldn't train or anything.'

The injury came at a bad time, just when Craig was making a name for himself at Villa. He first really caught the eye when the Villa lads reached the final of the FA Youth Cup against Middlesbrough. Both legs of the final were shown live on TV, and although Villa lost, Craig said, 'It was brilliant. A big crowd and everything. Brilliant. I was like, this is what I want to do!' The following season Craig was given several games in the reserves. It was a big step up, and meant playing with and against some famous players. He earned himself some good reviews. And then the injury happened.

'The coaches told me that a few years ago a knee injury like that would have ended my career,' he said, puffing out his cheeks and blowing out a big sigh just thinking about it. 'But now a club like Villa makes sure you get the best doctors and the best treatment, and they told me I would get over it. And I did.' The injury happened in February. It was not until just before the end of the season, in May, that Craig returned to the reserve team. 'The first few times I played, after working my way back to fitness, were a bit scary. I was like, will it hurt? Will it be OK? Will I be able to tackle or take a kick on it? But it held up so I just got on with it.'

For young pro footballers, getting on with it has changed a lot since academies were started. For years, kids who left school to join football clubs were used as cheap labour. They did all the painting and odd jobs that needed doing, cleaned all the boots, swept all the dressing rooms, and so on. Now, although there is still some boot cleaning to be done, the academies have to obey strict rules. They have to take good care of the boys, and they must take their training seriously. They have a set number of coaches, a welfare officer, a training officer, and rules to prevent the boys playing too many games. One day a week the boys go to college to learn IT or other skills. 'In case you don't make it,' explained Craig. Again, I could see the look of pain and worry on his face as he said it.

The Villa training ground, where their academy is based, is tucked away among farms and golf courses in the countryside. But none of the nearby land can be as well tended as Villa's training pitches. There is not a divot or a weed anywhere. When I visited, the young men of the academy were finishing lunch in the small, spotlessly clean food hall. The menu was all healthy stuff, of course. They seemed like any bunch of teenagers, except that they all looked in really good shape and were wearing white polo shirts with the club's badge on them. Most of them were destined to have their dreams dashed. They would be 'let go' by the club and returned to the real world. Only a handful of those boys picking at their pasta – perhaps only one, perhaps none – would get into the first team and become rich.

'Of course you think about the money some-times, when you see the first-team players coming in in great cars,' said Craig, 'but more than anything you think about playing foot-ball. I would still want this chance even if there was no money involved. We do know we are the lucky ones to have this chance. My friends outside the club tell me I am lucky.

'I still see lots of my old friends from school. I see as much as I can of them, but I don't go out drinking. I just won't go. I don't miss it or anything, because I would not do anything that might stop me playing as well as I can.

'I know my parents and family are proud of what I have done so far, and I am proud as well, but I've got a long way to go. A long way . . .'

Craig's voice trailed off again, and he straightened the leg that had been so badly injured.

'Thank you,' he said when I announced that we were finished. He asked if he had 'done all right'.

Anxious, again.

CHAPTER THREE

Jan Kozlowski, Stadium Manager

FOOTBALL GROUNDS ARE ODD places on days when there is no match. All those empty seats facing that empty patch of grass. The missing players and fans make it feel abandoned, like a ghost town.

There was something else missing at the Reebok Stadium when I went to meet Jan Kozlowski. The Reebok, of course, is the home of Bolton Wanderers Football Club, but the big sign on the huge wall said 'Bolton Wanderers oot all Clu'. The F and two Bs were missing. Jan knew all about the broken sign and made a joke about 'the eff 'n' bees'. But he did not smile. It is his job to make sure the eff 'n' letters are replaced as soon as possible. 'It is always getting broken,' he said, with a weary sigh. 'Kids play

22

football outside the ground and try to hit the signs. They don't mean to damage them, I don't think, but they often do.'

Jan is in charge of the stadium, and a glimpse into his life proves that there is so much more to football than what happens on the pitch. In fact, in the reception area at the Reebok, with its granite floor tiles and blue glass walls, you would think you were in a hotel or conference centre. And you are. The Reebok has a hotel and conference rooms. The hotel is built into one of the stands and some of the bedrooms overlook the pitch. So you could hold your wedding reception at the Reebok and then spend your honeymoon in a room with a view of the pitch.

You could do, but your marriage might not last long.

Sit in that smart reception at the Reebok and watch people arrive. There is no sign of a tracksuit or a football. Instead, the men and women who arrive are wearing business suits and carrying briefcases. They file into the half a dozen rooms that have been hired for conferences and meetings. Jan calls it 'sweating the asset', which sounds disgusting. Or perhaps it sounds like the latest fitness craze. 'Come on now, sweat your asset!' But the 'asset' Jan is talking about is the Reebok. He makes it 'sweat' by ensuring that it is working as much and as often as possible.

Amir Khan's final fight as an amateur boxer was staged at the Reebok. He is the Bolton lad who became famous at the Athens Olympics. The fight was held in a large room which is usually a restaurant. Getting the room ready, and setting up everything the TV people needed, gave Jan some headaches. Of course, the man with the worst headache on the night was Mario Kindelan, whom Khan fought and beat. A month after the fight, the stadium was the venue for an Elton John concert. That brought more headaches for Jan — and not because the music was loud. 'We put on lots of concerts and usually create a dressing room in one of the stands,' he explained. 'But Elton wanted a special room built in the car park, so that is what he got. Lulu, who was supporting Elton, didn't make a fuss. She was happy changing in the stand.'

And it's not only young boxers and old rockers who keep Jan busy. We go down to the side of the pitch, to the area where the Bolton manager, Sam Allardyce, struts and shouts during games. Dozens of bits of chewing gum have been stomped into the ground. 'I get the gum cleaned off every couple of weeks or so,' Jan said. 'We have to use a power hose and a scraper. But during a game big Sam just keeps chewing. It's nerves, I suppose.'

Ah, we are talking about football at last!

'I know the football is the most important part,' Jan said. 'All the other stuff – all that "sweating the asset" – is to help the football side. All the things we do at the Reebok the rest of the week, and the rest of the year, are to help the football.' And when a match is on, Jan can't watch because he knows how much the result means to the club. Instead, he prowls around the stadium. 'I walk around making sure everything is all right. I am a director, so I had a seat in the directors' box. But I was never there so I gave it up.'

Matchday for Jan begins with him arriving at nine a.m. and stalking around the stadium a couple of times. 'I check that litter bins are empty, that toilets are clean, that there are plenty of toilet rolls. There are teams of people whose job it is to do all that, but I check as well.

And there are all the safety and security things to check. The first time we played Chelsea after they had been bought by Roman Abramovich, the very rich Russian, I heard a rumour that his people would be armed. So I asked them. The last thing you want is someone pulling out a pistol or something. They assured me they had no guns. But when you looked at them you thought they probably didn't need guns.'

Safety and security is a big part of Jan's job. 'During the match I will spend time in our control room, where the police direct their people and where we can watch all our closed-circuit TVs. I have two radios and my mobile phone, and I am always talking to stewards. The only time I see any of the game is when I am in the control room, but then I might get called away to a toilet.'

Pardon?

'You might get a blocked toilet, either because of a plumbing problem or, shall we say, foul play. People tend to stuff roll after roll of toilet paper down the toilets. Don't ask me why. Anyway, we have a stand-by team of joiners, plumbers and workmen to mend toilet doors if they get kicked off, or whatever.'

How did Jan get such a glamorous job in football? He is a fifty-something chap with neat, short hair and a Lancashire accent. He went to Salford University and became an engineer. He worked in London for a while 'but didn't like it down south', so he moved to Chester and worked his way up in a big firm of builders. Eventually Jan was put in charge of some of their major building projects. But before you can build anything, sometimes you have to knock things down – and Jan demolished two of English football's most holy shrines.

'I was contract manager for the new Kop at Liverpool and the new Stretford End at Manchester United, and I had to knock down the old ones,' he said. 'There was a lot of history involved, and when I turned up for the demolition of the Kop we had to remove some devout fans who wouldn't leave the area. Mind you, I was responsible for building the new stands too, not just knocking down the old ones.'

It was while Jan was working for the builders at the Reebok that Bolton asked him to work for them instead. Before the stadium was built, there were only fields. Now, as well as the football ground, there is the Bolton Arena, a retail park, offices and a new railway station. But the Reebok dominates the area. If you see it, think of Jan making it 'sweat'. And think of him sweating himself as he scuttles off to find someone to mend those eff 'n' bees.

CHAPTER FOUR

Alan Curbishley, Manager

A TAILOR WAS AT Charlton's training ground when I arrived, fitting all the players for their Hugo Boss club suits. 'They are a strange shape,' he said, 'not like most men. Broad shoulders and chests. Little waists. Big thighs.' When I told my wife this later that day, she went very quiet for a while and then just said, 'Mmm.'

Curbs, as everyone calls Alan Curbishley, looked in good shape as well, when his suit fitting ended and he sat down in his football kit for our chat. It was the first week of pre-season training, but obviously he had not spent the short summer break eating chips. Had he enjoyed his holiday? 'Well, you don't get to go to the airport, fly away to the sun for two weeks and get away from it all. It's not like that. You have to leave your mobile on and you have to answer it. People want to contact you. People want to sell players and buy players.

'For instance, we went to Majorca this year and one night when we sat down for our evening meal my mobile went off. It was another manager. So I walked away from the table into the street. When I got back to the table, the starter had come. The others had eaten theirs, but before I could tuck in the mobile went again and I went away again. When I came back, my starter had gone because the others were all on their main course. My main course was there too, but then my chairman rang, so I walked away again. When I got back and sat down, the phone went again. This time it was an agent about a player I wanted. So I walked away again, and when I came back they'd had to take my meal away. That is what happens.'

No wonder he didn't put on any weight over the summer! And, as if to make his point for him, at that moment his mobile rang. He went off to try to sort out another transfer.

Charlton's training ground and academy are inside the M25 but outside the packed, urban areas of central London. If you think of the

M25 as a clock face, then Charlton's training ground and academy are where the number four is. And Curbishley is there at all hours. But, he said, 'I don't want it to sound as if I am complaining. We do get very well-paid. And lots of people work hard and don't get much spare time. I really am not complaining.

'What I am saying is there is just no getting away from it. We went to Minorca as well on our holiday. We went out for a meal one night and a guy came in with his girlfriend. He looked at me but he didn't say anything. The next night we went out for another meal, in this place in the middle of nowhere. The same bloke comes in. He goes, "I bit my lip last night, but I have got to say something tonight because I'm a Charlton season-ticket holder in the East Stand." So we had a chat about players and everything. That may sound like it is no big deal, and of course I don't mind talking to fans, but it's just that there is never any getting away from the job or from football. Even in the middle of nowhere. It is just part and parcel of my life.'

As for being able to switch off during the season itself – well, forget it. Charlton even go to their training ground on Sundays. The players have a 'warm down', and Curbishley and his coaches watch a video of the previous day's match. The players get Tuesdays off, but Curbishley usually goes to a match somewhere. He also goes to games on Monday and Wednesday nights. 'And sometimes I fly abroad on a Sunday to a game in Italy or somewhere, and back that night. So Thursday is the only night I am pretty sure I'll be at home. Most days I leave home at about seven in the morning and don't see any of my family. On a night when I go to a game I might not get home until after everyone has gone to bed. The biggest pressure I have got is that I have missed out on my kids growing up. I have missed it all.'

He described himself as being 'out of the loop'. 'I never watch any telly, except Teletext, to see what is happening in football. If I am in and *Coronation Street* is on, I don't know who half the characters are. I'll say, "Who's that?" and my family will say it's not worth trying to tell me. I've missed out on things like fishing too. I never took my boy fishing so we don't know if he would have liked it or not. Some people might say I have done him a favour. It has been my choice, though. And, although my kids have missed out on some things they have gained in others. But you do find that you get into your car in the morning and you are worrying straight away about your footballers instead of your family.'

For someone who cares so much about his team, Curbishley always seems very calm during and after matches. He is not a ranter and raver. But he wasn't always Mr Cool. 'No, I wasn't,' he said. 'I got sent off early in my career as a manager because I was going mad on the touchline. I got done by the FA. Then, soon after, we played at Arsenal and I noticed that Arsène Wenger [the Arsenal manager] and everyone on the Arsenal bench just sat there in the dug-out all afternoon. So after the game, I asked Pat Rice, their assistant manager, "What was all that about?" He said that Arsène thinks that if managers jump up and down and rant and rave or whatever, it has no effect. But when he wants to jump up and down about something it does have an effect because it is so rare.

'I thought about that. As a player, I had managers who would throw cups about when things went wrong, but after the fifth time you take no notice. So after that I decided I wasn't going to get too high and wasn't going to get too low. I actually have to tell myself to calm down, but I keep it like that. I like to think that if I am going to say something after the game, I can get it right. I will never criticize a player until I am 100 per cent sure of what happened. So if a goal has gone in, I might wait until I've seen the match video, perhaps on the Sunday. Then when I say something, the player knows it's not just me being angry. And he has calmed down after the game as well.'

So, if Curbishley thinks about football – about Charlton – all the time, but keeps it all inside him, bottled up, does he sleep well? 'No, not really. I have bouts when I am good, but I have bouts when I am bad. Someone told me that when you are lying awake at night, 99 per cent of your thoughts are negative. So I try desperately not to think about football if I am lying awake. But, yes, I do lie awake, even when we are doing all right.'

Some of that pressure comes from the fact that Charlton have to compete with clubs with much more money. Some of it comes from fans who expect Charlton to get better every season.

Some comes from knowing that however hard he works, all his efforts can be unpicked by a bad bounce of the ball or a dodgy refereeing decision. Curbs copes with this pressure by making himself stay calm, but how does it affect his family?

'There was one time a bloke said to my kid after school, "Charlton are having a bad time, and if your dad isn't careful he is going to get the sack." My kid told me this. So the next day I went up the school and had a word with this bloke, who was a plumber. I said to him, "Do me a favour. If you put in a poxy central heating system and get the sack, nobody at this school will know. But I can't be like that. Everyone knows my job. So I don't need people having a go at my kids. I know you said it jokingly, but we don't need it." That's what I told him.'

It seemed to me that, having agreed to talk about his life for this book, Curbs had decided to let out some of the stuff he keeps bottled up most of the time. But several times he repeated, 'I am not complaining.' He added, 'There are good friends of mine in football, good people, who were managers and lost their jobs and are desperate to get back in. Desperate. So it can't be such a bad life.'

It certainly has its compensations. Like a made-to-measure Hugo Boss suit, and being in shape to fit it well. Curbs has made his bed, as the saying goes, and he knows it is a king-sized bed in a very nice house. It's just that he doesn't get to spend much time in that house.

CHAPTER FIVE

Natasha Egan, Mascot

IT'S SATURDAY AFTERNOON, AN hour before kick-off. Plenty of fans are already in their seats, looking at their watches every few minutes. Down in the tunnel, one of the stars opens a changing-room door and calls over a security guard.

'Can you just check that I've got all my kit on, please?'

The guard, who goes through this routine with the star before every game, agrees.

Boots? Check.

Socks? Check.

Shorts? Check.

Shirt? Check.

Tail? Check.

Then Stamford the Lion jogs out onto the Chelsea pitch.

'I have to get a guard to check every week that I have got everything on,' Stamford explained. 'Because one week I forgot my shorts. I was out on the pitch and I was all excited. I was doing my job, you know, waving at the kids and signing things for them. Then, when I was halfway round the pitch, a little kid said, "Stamford! Where are your shorts?" Because my head is so big, I can't look down. But I felt my legs and he was right. I hadn't got my shorts on. I thought "NO!" and had to run off the pitch. After that kid noticed, everyone else did, and they were all laughing at me. I didn't go out onto the pitch again that day.'

The story of the Lion, the Pitch and the Wardrobe Malfunction is not as bad as it sounds because, of course, Stamford does not have all the bits of a real lion. That afternoon, the tail was the only thing sticking out. And anyway, under all the fake blue fur was Natasha Egan. Tash to her friends.

We met where she works during the week, at a toy shop in a shopping centre in the middle of one of south London's one-way traffic mazes. I don't know what I was expecting. After all, what sort of person dresses up as a big, blue lion? But I certainly wasn't expecting a slight, pretty twenty-six-year-old who looks at least ten years younger – who looks so delicate that you could blow her over. We went to a pub to chat, and I felt like I was with a superhero in her secret identity. First of all, I wanted to know how she became Stamford.

'Well, I used to work in the Chelsea shop – the Megastore – and one day the manager said "Does anyone want to be Stamford?" because the person who did it had left. It wasn't a matchday, but they wanted Stamford to walk around waving to all the people on tours of the ground. Everybody else was like, "You are joking!" But I thought, "Why not? It's just for one day." They said I did a good job. I didn't know how I could have been bad or good, you know, being a mascot, but that was eight years ago, and I'm still doing it. Actually, at first I shared the job with a friend of mine, a guy called Taff. So it was Taff and Tash.'

Natasha clearly remembers her first time out on the pitch because she was so nervous. 'They said, "Right, Tash, this is it now. Get your suit on, and get ready to go and do what you have got to do." But when I walked out and saw all the fans I was so scared. All I saw were all these little kids saying "Stamford! Stamford!" So I just started shaking everybody's hand. Then a little boy asked me to sign his programme, and I knew I was in trouble.

'I am not allowed to talk, so that people don't know it's only a little girly inside, and so that if I ever stop being Stamford the kids won't hear a different voice and work out that Stamford has changed. So I mimed writing something down and someone gave me a pen. But Stamford has a paw with three big fat fingers and a thumb, so I couldn't hold it properly. When I tried to sign it was just, like, terrible writing. But the little boy said, "Thank you! Thank you!" And after that everyone wanted me to sign stuff, so I did. After I got off the pitch, they said to me, "Right, you are going to be doing Stamford all the time." So I went home that night and tried to get my autograph right. I kept doing it and doing it, with a marker pen. I've got to the point where now I can do it easily with Stamford's paw.'

You see, even mascots have to practise. Well, they do if they take the job as seriously as Tash. She can't stop smiling, and what she does is certainly funny, but she takes it very seriously. 'I am so proud of what I do that I tell everybody,' she said. 'Usually, when I tell people they laugh, or people say, "Well, Tash, you are quite mad". But it is a really cool job to do.

'When I go on the pitch I do a little dance so that the kids know, by looking at it, that it is the same Stamford as last week, or last season even. If I see someone crying I will pretend that I am wiping tears away from my face. Or if they are happy I might put my thumbs up, or jump around with them. Also, I remember a lot of the children because they sit in the same place every week. I will go up to them and give them a big hug.

'There is one little girl called Chelsea who sits right in the front and is always in the same place. I know her name because one day I heard her mum telling her off a bit, saying, "Chelsea, you're not supposed to do that." But they didn't know I'd heard. So when she asked for my autograph I wrote "To Chelsea, love Stamford". And she was just made up. She was going, "Stamford knows my name! Stamford knows my name!"'

But it's not always all hugs and shaking

hands. 'Sometimes kids give me a playful punch,' Natasha said. 'With naughty kids, it is not playful. It hurts sometimes. And even the shaking hands gets a bit rough. Then there are the grown-ups who shake my paw. Because they think there must be a big bloke inside, they really give it a shake! And then there are the away fans who give me stick. Liverpool, Man U and Newcastle are the worst, for some reason. They chant "Who are yer?" and I think, "What is that about, having a go at a six-foot blue lion?" If the team hasn't been playing well, I even get stick from home fans sometimes. Don't ask me why. It is really quite weird. But the players are great to me. John Terry always pats me on the head. And when the teams come on it is my time to go off. I get changed and go and watch the game.'

Does she know any other mascots? After all, lots of them have the same middle name. There's Cyril The Swan (Swansea), Pete The Eagle (Crystal Palace), Splat The Cat (Norwich), Fred The Red (Manchester United) and Nelson The Dog (Portsmouth). 'There are sometimes races for mascots,' said Natasha, 'and we all get together. I won the race a couple of years ago, which was great. There were loads of other mascots and we got talking, and swapping stories. Fred The Red is very sweet. I liked him.'

So, who has the best costume? 'Stamford, of course,' Natasha replied. 'He's had a new one made. The only problem is that the feet are huge. I have to sort of plod along so that I don't trip over. I wear a Chelsea kit under the costume and there is a sort of frame inside Stamford's head which goes on my head. There is a little battery fan in there because it can get really hot. One summer, when there were six-a-side matches on at Chelsea and I was out in the heat all day, I lost loads of weight. I should call it the Stamford Diet. Getting dressed as Stamford takes about five minutes, and the hardest bits are the boots. They are so big that I have to keep my trainers on inside them. And then, when I have got it all on, I think, "I am now Stamford."

'I still get really nervous. I still think every week, "I can't do this." But once I'm out there with all the kids, with a really big crowd, I love it and I am part of it. Chelsea have Stamford because there is a lion in the club badge, so the way I see it is that I am on every one of the shirts worn by Chelsea fans. I think I want to do it for ever.'

So, if you are an away fan at Chelsea, don't give Stamford stick. Unless she forgets those shorts again.

CHAPTER SIX

Robbie Earle, Former Player

WHAT IS IT LIKE when it ends? What is it like, after eighteen and a half years as a pro footballer, when it is all over?

'When I finished playing, I couldn't change the pattern of my life which I'd had for so long,' said former Wimbledon midfielder Robbie Earle. 'I'd still have pasta for dinner on Friday and go to bed early. Then I'd wake up on Saturday with butterflies in my stomach ready for a game. But there was no game, nothing. It was the pattern, the routine, I was used to. My whole life and my family's life had been based around games. When the games stopped, I couldn't change the routine. What I had to do was get some mates almost to force me to go out for a beer on a Friday night to break that old pattern.' Since talking to Robbie, I've tried that

45

excuse – saying that my friends are forcing me to go out – but it hasn't worked. Just thought you should know, in case you are tempted to try it.

We met at a hotel near the Surrey gym Robbie uses nearly every day. I've known him since he started writing for a newspaper I used to work for. He is what us men call 'a good bloke'. He seldom answers his mobile, but never mind. He's good company – bright but never boring, interested in the views of others but with plenty of his own.

He joined Port Vale as a seventeen-year-old on a Youth Training Scheme. Nine years later, after more than 350 games for them, he went to Wimbledon in the top division. The phrase 'box to box' does not tell the whole story of his footballing career, but it was probably invented by someone who had Robbie's style in mind. Robbie would be in his own box one moment, stopping an attack, and then, when the ball reached the other end of the field, he would be in the other box, often scoring thrilling goals.

In 1998 he was made captain of Jamaica. When they reached the World Cup Finals that year, for the first time, the Jamaican prime minister declared a public holiday. Then, in the first game, against Croatia, Robbie scored the country's first ever goal in the World Cup Finals. That made him an instant and lasting hero. 'I could probably dine out anywhere in the Caribbean without paying,' Robbie said. He could probably dine out free in Stoke, near Port Vale's ground, as well. He might not want to eat in Stoke, but that's not the point. The point is that he was adored by fans of the teams he played for.

'And when all that ends, it is hard,' Robbie said. 'It is very hard. In fact, it is a scary time. From the age of sixteen, as long as you are doing OK, your football club takes care of you. Decisions are made for you.'

Once, he flew to a Jamaica game with another of the English-based players. At the airport a sign said 'go to gate such and such'. The other player had no idea what gates were or where they were. Every time he had gone anywhere, somebody had guided him. He'd never had to find his own way through an airport before.

'A lot of the things which are normal to other people are taken away from you in football so that you don't have to worry about anything

47

except playing,' Robbie explained. 'So when you are coming to the end of your career, all of a sudden you begin to wonder how you will cope. From the age of thirty-one or thirty-two I was thinking, "What am I going to do for the next twenty or twenty-five years? I'm still a young person." I wasn't only thinking about what I would do for money, I was wondering what I was going to do every day. There are a million good things about being a footballer, but the one downside is that it finishes so early.'

For Robbie, the end came suddenly, and it was painful. Wimbledon had new owners from Norway, and a new manager from the same country, Egil Olsen. He and Robbie fell out, and Robbie was dropped. In a reserve game at Watford, the goalkeeper fell on him and kneed him in the stomach. Robbie played on but later learned that he had ripped his spleen. Then he got an infection in hospital and almost died.

'I realized I wasn't going to play again,' he said. 'I wasn't ever going to run out at Old Trafford or line up against Liverpool again. It was over. The injury and illness made the decision for me. That made it a lot more sudden and a lot more harsh. And the hard thing is that the game goes on. You think, "Hold on, I'm not part of this any more." Wimbledon were still playing, Manchester United were still playing, but I wasn't. The TV coverage goes on and the headlines go on. A short while ago I had been making some of those headlines. But then, suddenly, everything goes on without you. It is a strange and lonely feeling.'

Plenty of players drift down the divisions or play show-biz matches. Not Robbie.

'I don't play at all now. Not in charity games, nothing. I am one of those people who are all or nothing, and I decided it would have to be nothing. My game was based on physical stuff – putting people under pressure, winning the ball, getting into the box, rushing around. But if I tried to do that in charity games people would tell me to calm down. I can't play calmed down.'

Robbie certainly appears very calm off the pitch. And he has made a new life for himself, as a pundit on TV and radio. But it was the abrupt end to his life as a footballer that interested me. One minute he was like a gladiator in an arena, the next it was over. That sudden change doesn't happen in many other walks of life. Except, I suppose, for gladiators. They were eaten by lions. 'You don't get eaten in football,' Robbie agreed, 'but the end does happen very quickly. And the calls stop. One minute the phone is ringing all the time with people asking you to do something, and then the calls stop and you realize that for all those years those calls were made because of what you were doing, your job, not really because of you.

'There is a lot to deal with for someone who is still quite young. There is a danger with some players that if you can't find something very quickly which fills your life and gives you highs, you can go off the rails in some way or another – drink or gambling or something. Or you can lose your money by investing in something – anything – which you think will give you something to do and give you those highs.'

Surely, I wondered, Robbie cannot miss all the schoolboy pranks that went on at Wimbledon?

'It is quite nice not having all the stuff which used to happen there. I was part of what they called the Crazy Gang. That meant having the tyres taken off your car, or having your clothes burned as a joke. But I even miss that. I miss the things that happened with a group of people who all got on with each other and were all trying to achieve success together.'

And then he said something which I think I should tell the police.

'We still meet twice a year – at Christmas and once in the summer. We go to a nice restaurant or a nice hotel. You can either have lunch and a couple of drinks and go, or you can take a first-aid kit and stay for the full twelve hours! As soon as we sit down together, the old feeling comes back, because we shared things and did things together.

'For instance, we played at Bolton once and they tried to psych Wimbledon out by leaving us waiting in the tunnel for about five minutes before the game. It was a big mistake. Jonesy [Vinnie Jones] said, "These people are trying to wind us up, but they ain't good enough." When we finally got out onto the pitch, we really got into them. For twenty minutes it was like an episode of *Casualty*. Now, when all us old players get together, someone only has to say "Bolton" and we all remember that day. It was something we all shared. A bit like being in the army together, I suppose.'

51

Does he have any regrets about his career?

'Now, when I look back, I think I would have liked to have had a go at a bigger club, and I am also disappointed about one game. It was an FA Cup semi-final against Chelsea in 1997. We were a good Wimbledon side, sitting well in the league, and we could play. The semi-final was at Highbury. It was a warm day and I was ready, ready, ready. I was up for it. But when I got out there I just felt from the first minute of the game that I wasn't right. I had built it up too much for myself and I wasn't right. I had nothing in me. I was the club captain, and I was that close to an FA Cup Final. It was my biggest domestic moment and my biggest domestic disappointment. For a week I was numb.

'But I can't really have any regrets. When I was a YTS boy at Port Vale I was very friendly with Mark Bright, and we used to say that it would be great if we could play in the second tier of football – the level just below what is now the Premier League. We used to say, "Wouldn't that be great?" But we both did quite a lot better than that. It is difficult when it ends, but when I look back, my career wasn't too bad really.'

CHAPTER SEVEN

Martin Tyler, Commentator

THE ANSWER MARTIN TYLER gave to my final question was very revealing. At the end of two pleasant hours nattering about his job and the strange way he'd got it, I asked, 'Would you have swapped it all for playing?' Without pausing, he replied, 'I would have swapped it all for one Premier League game.' So, Martin Tyler would much rather have played one game of top-level football than make a decent living talking about it on the telly. I think that is why he has been such a success. He loves the game, and he takes that love with him every time he goes to work.

Martin's voice has been part of football's soundtrack for more than thirty years and a major part of every fan's life. Close your eyes and you can hear him saying 'Shearer!' In fact, people come up to him when he is off duty and ask him to say just that.

Yet all he really wanted to do was play the game.

We had our chat at the same hotel at which I met Robbie Earle. They live near each other in Surrey. Martin was much fussier about what he had to eat, though. 'I went to university in Norwich,' he told me at the start of our meeting. 'Then I did another degree so that I could keep playing for the Uni team. Even after that I stayed in the area so that I could keep playing for them as an old boy. I just stayed in full-time education as long as I could to keep playing football.

'But in the end I ran out of money. I got a job in market research and moved to a flat in south London with Bob Willis, who I'd been to school with. He went on to be a top England cricketer, and then a cricket expert for Sky. But we were just two young blokes who played football together. We played for Corinthian Casuals in what is now the Ryman Premier League. It was a good league, and I played against good players and good teams. I was a very slow striker. I could head the ball, but I couldn't really run.

Bob was the goalkeeper. One game, at Barking, we lost 4–0, and they even chipped the ball over Bob for one of the goals, which took some doing when you see how tall he is. He kept letting them in, and I kept kicking off.'

Bob Willis was already having some success as a cricketer by that time. One morning in December 1970 he rang Martin to tell him that he had been called up to fly out to Australia and join the England squad. 'We had watched the first Test on a black and white TV in our little flat,' Martin recalled, 'and by the end of the series Bob was playing and helping England win the Ashes.'

What Martin described as 'Bob's rags to riches tale' inspired him, and he began to think he should do something with his life too. 'A girlfriend got me to phone a company who were going to bring out a football magazine. I rang up, got an interview, and somehow got a staff job – probably because they thought I knew about football. The job meant I got to work with some top writers, and to go to London Weekend Television to get pictures for pieces I was doing on skills and tactics. It was a Monday to Friday job, so I could still play football. I was happy. But then the mag ended and they offered me another job – on *Golden Hands*, which was about sewing. I said, "Thanks, but no thanks." '

The sewing world's loss was television's gain. 'London Weekend Television rang and offered me a job behind the scenes on their football programme, but again I said, "No thanks, because I want to keep playing." I was also doing some writing work for Jimmy Hill at the time and he told me I was mad. So I took his advice, rang LWT back and took the job – although it meant working on Saturdays, and that meant I had to stop playing. I was very upset.'

On his rare Saturdays off he went to whatever match LWT were covering. He just wanted to watch football. Eventually, he asked the director to let him take a tape recorder to the game and have a go at a commentary. The tape was not for broadcast, but the director liked it. 'Then, by luck, Southern TV rang up because their guy was covering tennis and they needed someone to do a match for them. LWT suggested me. I did another test tape first, and then the game for Southern. So the third match I ever did was a real broadcast.'

That was 1974, and the match was South-
ampton against Sheffield Wednesday, but what
Martin didn't say is that he must have been
good to get the chance in the first place, and
very good to make the most of it.

He told another story which sounds like luck,
but isn't really. 'Southern TV didn't do many
games, but they asked me to cover Brighton
against Mansfield, so I went to see Mansfield
play at Rotherham for research. There I bumped
into the head of Yorkshire TV sport, who
offered me a job a few weeks later. That was a
step up the ladder.' Yes, but the Yorkshire TV
bloke must have been impressed to see that
Martin was keen enough to go to Rotherham in
his own time.

After Yorkshire TV came a spell with
Granada, and then in 1990 Sky, who sat Martin
next to former player Andy Gray at matches. 'I
have worked with Andy Gray for fifteen years
now,' Martin said. 'You get less than that for
murder.'

And what does Martin do when he is not
sitting next to Mr Gray at a game? 'Well, I help
with my son's team. I go to his game on a
Sunday morning if I can, although I sometimes

have to leave before the end and go to work. And for the last ten years I have coached the local primary school on Mondays. On Tuesday or Wednesday I am probably working for Sky at a game. If it's an away game in the Champions League, of course that means travelling. On Thursdays I go training with my son. I help out and I join in. I love it. On Fridays I try to go to a Premiership training ground because that helps with the most important part of my job – getting the names of players right during games. And then on Saturday I'll do a game for Sky. I am also vice president of Woking Football Club, and I try to spread the word for them. One of my mates is involved at Walton and Hersham FC and I try to help him by finding out about the opposition.'

So, to recap, that is football every day of the week then, Martin.

'Erm, yes. Oh, and I still play if I can.'

Pardon? He still plays? Most media men have long since stopped dragging their pot bellies around football pitches. The only exercise most of us get is jumping to conclusions. We think a balanced diet is holding a burger in both hands. Yet Martin watches what he eats and still plays.

'I played for Woking reserves the other week,' he said. 'I was only meant to go on for a few minutes as a sub, just to say I'd done it, but they gave me the number nine shirt and I played all game. I couldn't run when I was twenty-five, so I suppose it doesn't make much difference that I can't run now that I am fifty-five.'

Even the thickest interviewer would have worked something out by now. Martin Tyler loves football. Some people who work in TV, radio or newspapers get fed up with the endless list of matches they have to cover. It shows in their work. But Martin is never bored, and that shows as well. But he would have swapped it all for just one Premier League game.

CHAPTER EIGHT

Steve Bennett, Referee

THE FIRST THING YOU notice when you spot a group of top referees together is that they all look so fit. During matches, they seem a lot older and a good bit slower than the super-fit young men buzzing around them. They look a good bit fatter as well. But when you visit the hotel at Daventry in the Midlands where Premier League refs gather once a fortnight, they all look lean and honed compared with the ordinary blokes at the hotel. The refs are in their forties, yet you would back them in a race against any one of these people milling about at the hotel.

These refs have to wear branded 'leisure clothing' – tracksuit trousers and polo shirts with a sponsor's name on them – which would look grim on most forty-somethings. But the referees get away with the look.

Ever since our top refs turned pro in 2001 they have all had their own training plans and special diets. They don't have beer guts straining at the material. Their fitness is tested at the Daventry sessions, and it's not the only thing that is checked. Every move a referee makes in a match is recorded by a system called ProZone. At Daventry, all those moves are picked over and talked about by all the other referees.

Few people know about the amount of work now done by refs before and after games. One top referee once told me, 'Even my best friends think I turn up with my boot bag just before kick-off, ruin somebody's weekend, and then go home again.' Steve Bennett said, 'No, that's wrong. We turn up several hours before kick-off and *then* ruin everybody's weekend!'

Refs consider every detail of their job. Steve even thinks about how he stands. 'If you stand with your feet side by side when players are coming at you to have an argument, you can be rocked backwards and start being backed away. So I stand with one foot slightly behind the other. And you don't start wagging your finger or pointing. You use the flat of a palm to say

61

"calm down". So my arm comes up with the flat palm, which says, "This is my space". I don't make eye contact, because that can be seen as aggressive. It's about managing the players and managing the situations.'

Steve learned some of those skills as a young man in the Winston Kent League. 'Once, when Deale were playing Hythe in a local derby with both teams fighting for the league, one player, who was known as a real Jack the Lad, gave a linesman dog's abuse. I had to send him off. No choice. But he said, "I ain't going. You'll have to abandon the game." So I said, "That's up to you, but it will all be on your head." And with that I walked away and took up my place for a corner. Well, he did go off, but not without walking past me and saying, "I'll effing get you after the game. I'll get you." In the dressing room afterwards I found that all my clothes had been dumped in the shower. But I couldn't prove anything.

'Another time in the Kent League, I was doing another local derby and from the dug-out comes a shout: "Referee, you are a clown!" Everyone heard it. I couldn't ignore it, so I walked over slowly and sat on the bench. They all looked at me. I said, "Guys, I am not a clown, but I can do magic. If my card comes out, you'll all disappear." So they all laughed, everyone calmed down, and there was no more trouble. At the end we all shook hands.'

In fact, more often it is referees who disappear. Every year, plenty of keen young lads and less young dads become refs. But most of them give up very quickly, driven away by the abuse they get when they start trying to control games on parks and playing fields. I am one of those park refs and the worst moment for me came when a lad threatened to bite off my ears. Sometimes the abuse is so bad, I wish he had.

Steve became a referee to improve his C.V. and help his career as a teacher. He was a good cricketer and a less good footballer, but he found that he was a very good ref. 'You start to be assessed as a referee and you get comments like "could referee at a higher level", so you try the higher level,' he said. It took Steve eleven years to work his way up from the Winston Kent League to the Football League. Then it took another four to become one of twenty Premier League refs. And it was three years after that before he reached the elite list of FIFA international refs.

Steve is now at the very top of his profession. In any other walk of life, someone who had climbed so high would win respect. But a referee gets ninety minutes of abuse from the crowd and backchat from the players, and then gets criticized on radio and TV and in the papers. 'As a ref, only those who are in the worldwide "family" of referees can have any feeling for the level I am at,' said Steve. 'The media is a very powerful tool and what is said is believed. And the media says we are all wrong. So the public out there think we are all wrong all of the time. Mind you, most people think that anyway, without the media. We are about as popular as traffic wardens. We make honest decisions during a game, but the fans see it differently because it affects their team. So you get them ringing phone-ins and ranting and raving.'

So referees have people yelling at them during matches and then fans complaining about them on radio after games. It must be hard to ignore it all and impossible to unwind.

'We are taught how to block out the crowd

during a game, but you are still buzzing, still thinking about everything, as you drive home. My wife will say, "How did it go?" I will say "OK" or something, but not really go into details. I try not to take my work home, in that respect. And I don't have Sky TV and I don't read the papers, because you cannot let the stick get to you.'

When referees went pro, Steve gave up teaching, but one of the many stories he tells about his new career proves what a thankless job it is. At the start of the 2004/05 season, FIFA, the game's law-making body, decided to stop players taking off their shirts to celebrate goals. In England, referees held meetings to tell clubs about the new law and sent a poster to every team. The poster showed Tim Cahill, of Everton and Australia, whipping off his top, and made it clear that stripping like that was now banned. One month into the season, Steve refereed an Everton game and took Cahill's name for a nasty foul. Later in the match, Cahill scored – and took off his shirt to celebrate, just like in the poster. 'I had to book him again,' said Steve, wincing at the memory. Because two yellow cards make a red, Cahill was sent off.

And who do you suppose was blasted by TV, radio, papers, outraged fans and an irate manager? FIFA, for making the new law? The player, who took no notice of a poster in which he had starred? Everton, for not making sure he knew the rule? No, it was all the ref's fault. 'According to everyone, it was my fault that he got sent off,' said Steve, shaking his head. 'The media said I'd sent him off for taking off his shirt. But I sent him off for getting two cautions. They all said I should have shown "commonsense", but if I had not booked him that would not have been fair on anyone else anywhere else in the country who was booked for taking off his shirt.' Steve shook his head and winced again.

Which brought me to the question referees are asked most often. No, it's not 'Are your parents married?' It's 'Why do you do it?' Why would anyone wish to run twelve kilometres during a match, make a big decision every thirty seconds or so, and then have their efforts discussed by 'experts' who often do not know the laws of football?

'For me it is about being involved in football,' Steve said. 'And about challenging yourself.

When it goes well, when you finish a game and you know it has gone well, it does feel as if you have really done something.' But how do you deal with situations like the Cahill shirt affair, when the entire world thinks it's your fault? Or having your clothes put in the shower? 'You work your way through it. You deal with it. Deep down you know when you are right or if you have made a mistake. And if you know in your heart of hearts that what you have done is correct, then you can park it and move on. In those two cases, I knew I had done the right thing. Nobody else seemed to know it, but I didn't lose any sleep over them.'

That seemed a good moment to end our interview, and Steve and I went off to have lunch with the other refs. It was a light lunch, all pasta and no fried stuff. But I was forced to think, recalling what Steve had said, that perhaps refs do have strong guts after all.

CHAPTER NINE

Skylet Andrew, Agent

HAVE YOU HEARD THE joke about the footballer of the year who won a little bronze statue? His agent took an arm and a leg.

In the list of people we don't like, football agents are near the top, along with tax men. Oh, and referees. Trying to keep an open mind about Sky Andrew, a well-known agent, was not helped by the months it took to arrange a meeting. When I rang his mobile, he was always driving – except for the time when he said, 'I'm with a manager and a player at the moment, trying to do a transfer.' When we did, finally, arrange to meet, things did not go to plan. His PA rang me twice to put the meeting back to later in the day. And even then, when I got to his office he was not there.

Agents are busy, busy, busy.

It gave me a chance to nose around the room, though. The TV was on, with *Big Brother Live* showing, and a PlayStation was plugged in. On the walls were pictures of his clients, a white-board crowded with events and dates, and a poster saying 'Attitude is a little thing that makes a big difference'.

Sky's attitude made a big difference when he hurried in. He was very cagey. Perhaps he had heard that I liked to tell the joke about the arm and the leg. I asked what he'd been up to all day. 'We've got a number of things on at the moment,' he replied.

Not very revealing.

It was not until much later that he relaxed and smiled – a big, warm, really happy smile. That was when he started talking about Stuart Nethercott – and that tells you a lot about Sky and about some other agents.

In the early 1990s, two young men were being touted as the next big things at Spurs. They were certainly both big – two large centre-halves. But it turned out that only one of them had a big future. Sol Campbell went on to fame and fortune, but the other one, Nether-cott, went on to Maidstone, Barnet, Millwall,

Wycombe and Woking. Not much fame, and not much of a fortune. But both are still Sky's clients. 'Stuart is the best lad you will ever meet,' Sky said. 'A top, top lad. Yes, of course I still represent him.'

So it's not all about money then?

'If you chase money, money just puts on a pair of trainers and starts running,' Sky said, sounding like one of his posters. 'And besides, my mum would never let me make money my god. She was, and is, a real stickler for doing things right. Sometimes she annoys me how she insists on always doing the right thing. But she has made me think the same way. No matter what anybody says to me about anything, if I don't think it is right, I won't do it that way.'

Of course, he has made a few bob representing Campbell. Sky drives a Merc with a special numberplate. He grew up in Stratford, near Campbell, but he now lives in posh Potters Bar in Hertfordshire. But he is not flash. His clothes are nice but not showy. His office is clean and modern, but it is on the first floor of a house in an ordinary London suburb. And at the start he worked for Campbell for nothing.

'I played table tennis [he was Commonwealth

champion] and used to go for a week's training with the British team,' Sky said. 'Sol was at the national football school, and we used to meet in the queue for the food. He asked me to help him, and that was how it started – just to help a mate. I had never done anything like that before. But I had been very keen to promote table tennis. I had done everything I could to get the sport on TV and to get firms to support it. I'd had some pretty good results too.

'There was no contract with Sol to start with, and no money. I was helping my mate out full time. He was quite shy, and I would try to get him on things like judging panels at talent shows. He was on £250 a week at Spurs and drove an A-reg Ford Orion. When we went to jobs he used to park his car around the back somewhere so that nobody saw us arriving in it.

'We were just two people from working-class backgrounds. I mean, I come from a background where my mum worked very hard for her family. We were two boys making this journey together. And don't forget, nobody knew Sol would become the player he did. You can't pick out a seventeen-year-old and know for certain that he will be one of the best players in the world. But that is what happened, and we have helped each other.'

What does he actually do for Sol and his other clients?

'I've got fourteen clients,' Sky said, 'and if I spend ten days a year dealing with their contracts with their clubs, then that is a lot. The rest of the time it is support and advice. If one of them wants to buy a house then I will go and look around the area, look at houses, and so on. I'll get builders in or whatever. If they want a new car, I'll look at cars. I'll look at schools for their kids. I'll organize what my clients do, arrange events. Anything. Everything.'

In the early spring of 2005 Sky's client, Jermaine Pennant, was sent to prison. It was a tough time for both men, but, said Sky, 'That was when he needed to ring me and know I would help. He got three months. I sat there in the court, and then I made sure things were done right while he was in prison. I talked to Birmingham, where he had been on loan, and did a deal for him so that when he came out he could get back to playing football and get his life back on track. That is why I have only got fourteen clients. It's a close network. If something happens, you deal with it. In a big company, you might not be able to get hold of people. Or you might need someone else to make the decision. But this is my company, and I make the decisions. And my clients can get hold of me.'

Campbell's move from Spurs to their hated rivals Arsenal caused a huge row. Spurs got no money because Campbell's contract had ended. Campbell himself pointed out, 'I cost Tottenham nothing. I gave them everything for ten years of my life and I left them when my contract was up.' Sky takes the same view. 'Look, none of my clients has ever broken his contract,' he said. 'To me, that is important. And when people have a go at agents, they forget that.'

People certainly do have a go at them. Nobody has a good word for agents. Except players. Put yourself in the place of a player. A club wants you to sign for them. In the room, across the table from you, sit the manager, chairman and chief exec. They want you to sign a contract to work for them for four or five years. The contract has lots of pages and has been put together by a lawyer. You'd want someone like

Sky on your side, wouldn't you? And think about the transfer market. One club buys a player from another, like a farmer buys a prize cow. Again, you'd want Sky making sure you got your fair share of the deal, wouldn't you?

Of course, we don't read about the fair shares and the decent deals. We only hear murky rumours about dodgy deals. And, with so much money involved, there are certainly plenty of sharp operators. But Sky doesn't get upset about all the bad press. 'I don't think people mind if an agent has looked after the same player for a long time,' he said. 'Nobody can say I got hold of Sol to make money. Looking after one player for all that time, and having only a small number of clients, is not the way to make a lot of money.'

Then we started talking about Stuart Nethercott again, and Sky started smiling again. It is very clear that he represents Stuart because they are friends. Then his mobile and his office phone rang at the same instant. Time for me to go. Time for Sky to be busy, busy, busy.

I shook his hand on the way out and noted that I'd still got my arm and my leg.

CHAPTER TEN

Alistair Mackintosh, Chief Executive

THERE MUST BE SOMETHING in the tea at Manchester City. When Kevin Keegan was manager, he was famous for his drive and desire. Next came Stuart Pearce, a man who never sits down during a match. He is forever kicking and heading imaginary balls, or bouncing up and down like a ball himself. Alistair Mackintosh, the chief exec, is every bit as manic. He happily works at least six days a week and seldom takes a holiday 'because the job is like a holiday – I enjoy it so much'. He must do, because he turned down much more money in order to join the club.

Alistair was born in Manchester – or 'lucky enough to have been born in Manchester', as he put it – but he went to school in the New Forest and then on to university. He became an accountant and worked for two top firms in the City of London. Then, at twenty-eight, he applied for two jobs at the same time. One was at *The Economist* magazine, and the other at Maine Road.

He was offered both and chose the football job. *The Economist* said they would match whatever Man City were paying. 'I had to tell them that City were actually paying a lot less than them,' Alistair told me. 'They offered me an extra £10,000 to go to the magazine. Then another £10,000, and then another £10,000. I kept turning them down because I wanted to work in football, and I wanted to work for Man City. I decided it was a once-in-a-lifetime chance. It was a chance to work in football, a chance to do a job that is more than a job – a job I could live.'

That story is all the more amazing when you remember that at the time, in the late 1990s, City had dropped into the Second Division – football's third tier. Their ground, Maine Road, was getting tatty, and the club's finances were a mess.

Within nine months, Alistair had been

promoted to finance director and City were in the play-off final with a chance of going up into football's second tier. 'In that play-off at Wembley we were 2–0 down to Gillingham after ninety minutes,' Alistair recalled, 'and everyone near me was very unhappy. I knew – though they didn't – that if we stayed down a lot of those people would have to be made redundant. When we scored twice in injury time and went on to win on penalties, everyone near me went mad. But my joy was on a different level, and for a different reason.'

Alistair was promoted again, to managing director, and then to chief exec. I asked him what a chief exec does, but learned his job is defined by what he doesn't do.

We met at the City of Manchester Stadium, a huge, modern ground that you can see for miles. But Alistair hasn't given himself a posh office. It's a big enough room, but there are files and paperwork everywhere, and the view from the window is of the base of a floodlight pylon.

One thing he never does is go into the dressing room. 'That is the manager's area,' he said. 'I only go to areas where I can help or add value.' Alistair is fit and dapper enough to look like a footballer, but he doesn't try to be one of the lads. 'I speak to the manager each and every day. I keep him informed about what I am doing and he keeps me informed. But I am not someone who looks to make friends around the football club, especially on the playing side. That is because there may come a time when difficult decisions have to be made.' In other words, he doesn't make mates because he may have to sack them one day. That's a tough stance to take, in a tough business. 'I don't want to compromise the business,' he added. 'I am very focused on Manchester City Football Club.'

Any fair judge would say that he and City have been successful. 'Starting from that low base, in the Second Division, we have come a long way,' Alistair said. 'And if you look at some of the clubs who were level with us then who are still there, you would have to say we have done well. Now we have to try to do better.'

Alistair relaxes by going to rock concerts and watching Bournemouth play football. He started supporting Bournemouth when he was at school in the New Forest. He stands as a fan behind the goal whenever their games do not clash with City's. And he goes home every now and then. 'My wife would say I spend too much time at work, but I honestly feel so lucky. If on the first day of my career someone had said at fifty-five or something you will be on the board of Manchester City Football Club, I would have been delighted. Yet I was on the board here at twenty-eight. Sometimes the job is demanding. When we are buying or selling a player, the only time I am not making or taking telephone calls is for the few hours when I am asleep. But I could never say to my friends "I've had a bad day at work", because my work is going to Premier League matches, mixing with top players, and working in football. My friends would all love my job. And I love it.'

Surely things must get tough when the fans are unhappy? 'We have the most loyal fans,' Alistair said. 'We had average crowds of 28,000 in the Second Division. People put a lot of time and effort into supporting Manchester City. Unlike the high street, where they just go to another shop if they are unhappy, they cannot go elsewhere if they feel let down by us. All they can do, really, is complain, and when they do our job is to listen.'

All right, but what about the fact that all his planning and all his work can be undone by the bounce of a ball? Can Alistair really enjoy watching games? 'We look after the players and we have a "no excuses" policy, which means we don't want anything – whether it's the pitch, the car park or whatever – to give the manager or players anything to blame,' Alistair said. 'So when the game is on, I have done my job. All I can do is sit and watch. And yes, I enjoy it. I have the best seat in the house at a Premier League match. Of course I enjoy it.'

You see what I mean about there being something in the tea. Surely nobody is that full of beans without being full of something else.

Alistair has always been one of life's mad-keen blokes, but something happened once on the way back from a match which made him enjoy life even more. 'One of the biggest things that has affected me in the last few years was when we were coming back from a match at Portsmouth in 2004,' he explained. 'We'd lost 3–2, and all the board were flying back on a small plane. We all sat there moaning because we'd lost. Life could not be worse, we thought.

'Then, ten minutes into the flight, one of the

two propellers stopped. We fell about two thousand metres. Smoke started coming in. All the red lights went on and the pilot started saying, "Mayday! Mayday!" We thought we were dead. I can remember thinking about my mobile phone and whether or not to ring my wife to say I loved her, and goodbye. But would the mobile phone interfere with the plane's systems? We kept plummeting. We were looking out at this one propeller – all that was keeping us alive. When we got below the clouds and could see the lights, it was a fantastic feeling.' They eventually made an emergency landing at an airfield south of London.

Two things have happened as a result of this shocking drama. The first is that the Manchester City board no longer fly back from matches on small planes. The second is that Alistair now makes the most of every day. So, mystery solved. He is so darned full of life because he once came so close to death. But, just to be on the safe side, I didn't have any of the tea.

CHAPTER ELEVEN

Jamie Carragher, Player

MELWOOD. SOUNDS A LOVELY place, doesn't it? A quiet, restful, leafy clearing perhaps. Actually it's in a suburb on Merseyside. The streets which hem Melwood in on all sides are crammed full of terraced homes, and Melwood itself is surrounded by a six-foot concrete wall. On top of the wall are three lines of barbed wire. It could be an army barracks or a prison. But Melwood is the training ground Liverpool have used since before Bill Shankly made them a force in the land in the 1960s.

Then, the players changed at Anfield, the club's ground, and made the ten-minute journey to Melwood by team coach. But Melwood was rebuilt during Gerard Houllier's reign as manager. Now, as well as several pitches, there is a modern two-storey building which is about the size of a school. It houses a gym, offices, medical rooms, a media centre, kitchens, dining rooms, and big, airy dressing rooms.

The concrete and barbed wire are there just as a precaution, because people come from all over the world to see Melwood. Every day there are fans at the gate hoping for autographs. One fans' website helpfully points out that there are a few places where holes in that wall allow fans to gawk at what is going on inside.

So let's go inside. Let's drive past those fans at the gate and park. Let's walk beside flower beds to the two big, heavy, glass doors. We can walk across the slate floor, turn right at the reception desk and go into the media centre. At its heart is a big room with a high ceiling, like a school hall. This is where press conferences are held before matches. Today, a children's charity is collecting palm prints to sell. Steven Gerrard is having his hand covered in ink. Around the outside of this room are doors to smaller rooms, like little classrooms. Into one of them, looking chipper, bounces Jamie Carragher. He is wearing a T-shirt and combat trousers.

I wanted to know what Jamie's working life

was like, and we started with one of those long coach journeys to an away game. 'We have a decent-sized table at the back and a lot of the lads gather there and play cards,' he explained. 'Some lads like to sit on their own with their DVD players or iPods, and that's fair enough. But the majority of us – ten or twelve of us – get together at the back. We play for a bit of money, but not much. Not enough so that it matters to anyone if he wins or loses. Mostly we play to have a bit of banter, to pass a bit of time and get a bit of team spirit going.

'We also have a meal together on the night before a match and then get an early night. When I first got into the team, I used to spend a lot of time thinking about what a big game it would be the next day, but now I sleep OK. It is not so easy when you are playing a night game, though, because you go to your room in the afternoon and try to have a nap then. If you get a couple of hours' sleep then it really helps later on, but if you don't get to sleep in the first half an hour you probably won't get off. But as my kids get me up early when I'm at home, I usually don't have any trouble having a kip in the afternoon.'

That picture of normal family life changes when Carragher gets to the match. Then he becomes far from ordinary.

'Running out for the match is always special, always a buzz. Home games are the best because running out at Anfield is something special, especially at night games. For Champions League games and in the Premier League, you line up facing the stand before the game. That is when I have a look at the directors' box to see who is watching us. I listen to the Champions League music and try to take it all in.

'But once the game starts I am not aware of the crowd. Really. People always ask about that, but the honest answer is I am not aware of anything except the game. If the game stops you might notice the crowd, and you might hear a few comments – good or bad – if you go over to the line to take a throw-in. But generally you are concentrating so hard that you don't take anything else in. When we played Chelsea in the Champions League Semi-Final [in 2005], everyone said the atmosphere was amazing. I was certainly aware of it before the game, but actually during the game I couldn't tell you what it was like.

'Of course there are times when I can remember the crowd. I remember my debut at Anfield in 1997, against Aston Villa. I actually scored in that game – one of the few goals I've got. I remember the roar of the crowd when I scored. That stayed with me. When I went out that night I could shut my eyes and the noise would come back to me. But generally, if you're thinking about the crowd when you're playing, you can't be concentrating on the game.

'At half-time the boots come off straight away. The boots and the pads, to give my feet and calves a rest. We all have drinks but we don't say anything for the first few minutes. Then the manager talks to us and after that I might go around and talk to the other defenders about what we have got to do – and then it is out again.'

After a match, Carragher, like referee Bennett, cannot switch off. 'After a night game at home, the game is still going through your mind for hours. I'm usually on the phone to my friends talking about it – who played well, what happened and things. I'm often thinking about it for so long that I do have trouble sleeping. That is at home. It's strange, but away from home in Europe I don't have any trouble sleeping. Probably because we have been defending for ninety minutes and I'm so tired. You can't get away from it the next day either. You watch Sky, BBC, all the news, all the reaction, and read all the papers. I know some football players say they don't read the papers, but I don't believe them.'

Games come thick and fast and players must make sure they nurse their legs.

'The day after a game we come in to Melwood and have a twelve-minute run to get the legs moving again, and to use the steam room. Then it is probably time to start thinking about the next game, about who you will be up against. If he is a quick lad, I'll think about whether I am going to drop off him a bit. That sort of thing.

'I love training. I love being fit. I like to do something to get a good sweat on every day. I work hard, and then have a nice shower. It makes you feel clean and good. Mentally and for life, I think keeping fit makes me feel good. I think if I wasn't a footballer I would still have to keep fit.'

But Carragher is a footballer and I wondered

what the best parts of his life were. Fame?
Money?

'The best thing for me about being a
footballer is playing away from home in Europe
in famous grounds. You play at Juventus,
Barcelona or Roma, and you look around the
ground at the end of the game and take it all in.
Plenty of good footballers don't get to play in
these places. Oh yeah, that's the special bit. You
swap shirts and have a good look round. That
night in Istanbul, when Liverpool won the
European Cup, went by in a flash, but I tried to
soak it all in at the end. I have watched the
video lots of times and it does bring it all back.'

I wondered, as well, what was the worst part
of life at the top? 'The worst thing in football is
injury, and I'd say in some ways a small injury
is worse than a big one. That might sound
funny, but if you have a big injury you are out
and you have got to get yourself fit again. With
a small injury you can still play, even though
you are not quite right. It nags at the back of
your mind. The other thing that nags at the
back of your mind is getting old! I look at other,
older players in other teams, see if they have
lost any pace, and try to work out how much

longer I have got playing at the absolute top level.'

Later, I watched as Jamie drove out of Melwood. He stopped at the gate, rolled down his window and signed the books and photos that were being held out to him.

Jamie was the last person I talked to for this book. It just worked out that way. I chose Jamie because I knew he was proud of being an ordinary lad from Liverpool who just happened to be very good at football. But it was tough tying him down for a meeting because he was always playing, or travelling to and from games all over Europe.

As the fans mobbed his car, it struck me that in some ways, Melwood, with its walls, represents his life. Jamie is at a special time in his life, in a special place, and everyone would love to be there. The young Aston Villa player I talked to for this book, Craig Gardner, wants to be a top pro. Robbie Earle wishes he was still a top player. Martin Tyler, the broadcaster, wanted to be a player. And the rest of us are peering in at the lives of the players just like the fans peeking through the concrete wall at Melwood.

The Premier League and its clubs are committed to delivering schemes in local communities. Through investment in the Football Foundation, along with the Football Association and the government, hundreds of millions have been spent on improving grass-roots facilities. This has provided the chance for people of all ages and abilities to play the game.

The Premier League also runs a wide variety of programmes which aim to promote healthy living, offer educational and employment opportunities and reduce crime. These programmes include Premier League Reading Stars where all twenty clubs nominate a first-team player to be a Club Reading Champion who then selects his favourite adult or children's book. This list is then used via local public libraries to inspire families to read together.

WORLD BOOK DAY
Quick Reads

We would like to thank all our partners in the
Quick Reads project for all their help and support:

BBC RaW
Department for Education and Skills
Trades Union Congress
The Vital Link
The Reading Agency
National Literacy Trust

Quick Reads would also like to thank the Arts
Council England and National Book Tokens for
their sponsorship.

We would also like to thank the following
companies for providing their services free of
charge: SX Composing for typesetting all the titles;
Icon Reproduction for text reproduction; Norske
Skog, Stora Enso, PMS and Iggusend for paper/board
supplies; Mackays of Chatham, Cox and Wyman,
Bookmarque, White Quill Press, Concise, Norhaven
and GGP for the printing.

www.worldbookday.com

Quick Reads

BOOKS IN THE *Quick* Reads SERIES

The Book Boy	Joanna Trollope
Blackwater	Conn Iggulden
Chickenfeed	Minette Walters
Don't Make Me Laugh	Patrick Augustus
Hell Island	Matthew Reilly
How to Change Your Life in 7 Steps	John Bird
Screw It, Let's Do It	Richard Branson
Someone Like Me	Tom Holt
Star Sullivan	Maeve Binchy
The Team	Mick Dennis
The Thief	Ruth Rendell
Woman Walks into a Bar	Rowan Coleman

AND IN MAY 2006

Cleanskin	Val McDermid
Danny Wallace and the Centre of the Universe	Danny Wallace
Desert Claw	Damien Lewis
The Dying Wish	Courttia Newland
The Grey Man	Andy McNab
I Am a Dalek	Gareth Roberts
I Love Football	Hunter Davies
The Name You Once Gave Me	Mike Phillips
The Poison in the Blood	Tom Holland
Winner Takes All	John Francome

Look out for more titles in the *Quick* Reads series in 2007.

www.worldbookday.com